BODIES IN

CRISIS

LEARNING DISORDERS

Jacqueline L. Harris

Twenty-First Century Books

A Division of Henry Holt and Company
New York

Twenty-First Century Books
A Division of Henry Holt and Company, Inc.
115 West 18th Street
New York, New York 10011

Henry Holt® and colophon are registered trademarks of Henry Holt and
Company, Inc.
Publishers since 1866

Published in Canada by Fitzhenry & Whiteside Ltd.
195 Allstate Parkway, Markham, Ontario L3R 4T8

Printed in Mexico
All first editions are printed on acid-free paper.

Created and produced in association with Blackbirch Graphics, Inc.

Library of Congress Cataloging-in-Publication Data

Harris, Jacqueline L.
    Learning disorders / Jacqueline L. Harris. — 1st. ed.
        p.   cm. — (Bodies in crisis)
    Includes bibliographical references and index.
    Summary: Discusses how the brain processes information and examines the
emotional, biological, and physiological manifestations of various learning disorders.
    ISBN 0-8050-2604-5 (acid-free paper)
    1. Learning disabilities—Juvenile literature. [1. Learning disabilities.]
    I. Title. II. Series.
    RC394.L37H37 1993
    616.85'889—dc20
                                                              93-25910
                                                                 CIP
                                                                  AC

Contents

Most learning disabilities are first noticed during the early years of childhood. This is when the human brain acquires the capacity to learn about movement, senses, and language.

The Learning Process

Some people have difficulty learning. These people do not have physical disabilities like blindness or deafness, and their intelligence is often normal. Rather, they have severe problems with such things as remembering, thinking, and seeing and hearing correctly because their brains do not process information in the most effective way. People with these problems are learning-disabled, and their problems are usually referred to as learning disabilities.

Learning disabilities include problems that deal with mental processes—such as reading difficulties (dyslexia), writing difficulties (dysgraphia), difficulties in performing mathematical operations (dyscalculia), and difficulties in paying attention or concentrating (attention deficit hyperactivity disorder). They also include problems that people have in learning to use their bodies properly. These difficulties are called motor-control problems.

The following stories about two children with different types of learning problems show what can happen to people with learning disabilities. To understand the problems that each person must deal with, however, it is necessary to have some knowledge about the role that the brain plays in learning and the stages that a developing person goes through to learn. While the learning-disabled have problems learning, it does not mean that they cannot learn at all. Once doctors, counselors, and teachers determine what their problems are, they can help these people to learn and to control behavior patterns that sometimes result from certain disabilities.

Beth's Problem

Five-year-old Beth had a lot of trouble getting people to understand her. Often she couldn't think of the word she wanted. For *stove* she would say "the thing you cook on." Sometimes she'd say "hot" when she meant "cold." In kindergarten, her classmates called her a baby because she couldn't speak properly. As she grew older, Beth's poor memory for words produced more problems. She couldn't look at a word, know what it meant, and say that word. Beth couldn't learn to read. She couldn't write or spell properly either. While Beth knew what she wanted to say, she couldn't write it so others could understand her. When describing her vacation at the beach, Beth wrote, "The wivze wre hih. My brith and I dit guh n the watuh. We wer sacrd." (The waves were high. My brother and I didn't go into the water. We were scared.) Beth was suffering from a learning disability called dyslexia, the inability to read. Her inability to write is called dysgraphia.

Marc's Problem

Marc was a clumsy child. He spilled his milk, tripped over his own feet, and ran into walls. His parents hoped he would outgrow this behavior, but as Marc got older, it was becoming clear that he had difficulty with movement, or motor functions. He just didn't understand how his body fit into the world around him. He wasn't able to judge space—to tell where things were. Marc wanted to play baseball, but when he tried to hit the ball with the bat, he missed almost every time. He just couldn't figure out where the ball was. When he did manage to hit the ball, he couldn't find first base. Marc's problems with space also affected his ability to learn arithmetic. For example, he couldn't write the numbers in the proper places so he could get the right answer. When the teacher asked the class to add 10 and 1, Marc would line up the two numbers in the wrong places and would get 20 as his answer instead of 11:

$$
\begin{array}{r}
10 \\
+1 \\
\hline
20
\end{array}
$$

Marc had trouble doing the problem in his head, and when he wrote it down, he got it wrong. Marc's arithmetic learning problem is called dyscalculia.

Learning and the Brain

Information coming in from the senses—vision, hearing, smell, taste, and touch—is crucial to learning. The organs that control the senses, such as the eyes and the ears, are connected to the brain by chains of tiny cells called neurons (nerve cells). The brain itself is made up of a vast network of neurons. A neuron has a round nucleus (unit at the center of a cell) and a number of threadlike attachments or fibers. These fibers transport messages from neuron to neuron.

Messages, in the form of electrical impulses, travel from sense organs along neuron-to-neuron pathways to different parts of the brain. Neurons are not actually attached to each other. Messages are transmitted from neuron to neuron by chemicals called neurotransmitters. Neurotransmitters are made by the neurons, which spurt them across the gap to the next nerve fiber.

Learning takes place when an impulse travels to the brain from a sense organ such as the ear. When some-one says the word *cat*, for example, each part of the word is transmitted by a separate nerve impulse. Each word part is temporarily stored in the brain until the entire word has been transmitted. Then it is synthe-sized, or combined. As a result, we hear the word *cat*. Imagine that at the same time we hear the word *cat*, we are looking at a picture of a cat. Different bits of visual information about the cat—long tail, whiskers, fur—arrive in the brain and all come together there. We also look at the word *cat* as we look at the picture. Visual information about the word then arrives in the brain and

The Structure of a Neuron

A neuron (nerve cell) is made up of a cell body, a nucleus, and a number of branching projections called dendrites that bring impulses to the cell body. Every neuron has a taillike projection called an axon (the conducting fiber of a neuron). Axons vary in length from a fraction of an inch to several feet. An axon branches at its end to form terminals that send impulses to target cells. Impulses reach the target cells by means of chemicals called neurotransmitters, which travel to the cells across gaps called synapses. Bundles of the axons of many neurons are known collectively as nerves.

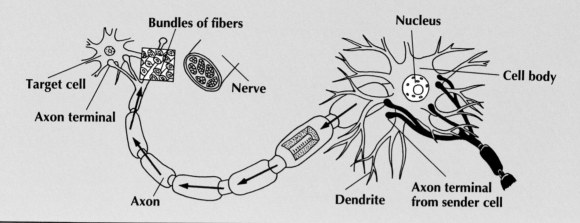

Bundles of fibers · **Nucleus** · **Target cell** · **Nerve** · **Cell body** · **Axon terminal** · **Axon** · **Dendrite** · **Axon terminal from sender cell**

How Neurotransmitters Work

When an electrical impulse travels down a nerve-cell axon, it causes the release of a chemical neurotransmitter at the axon terminals.

1. Impulse travels down neuron axon, from cell body toward axon terminals; neurotransmitter is released from tiny swellings, called synaptic knobs, at axon terminals.

2. Neurotransmitter crosses synapse (gap between axon terminal and receiving cell) to surface membrane of target cell, where it binds to a protein called a receptor.

3. If sufficient target-cell receptors are activated by neurotransmitter binding, an impulse is initiated and passes, in turn, down target cell's axon.

Example of neurotransmitter activity Neurotransmitters enable the pupil to change size in different light conditions.

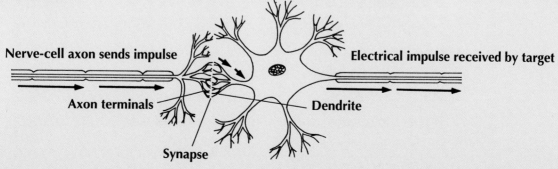

Nerve-cell axon sends impulse · **Electrical impulse received by target** · **Axon terminals** · **Dendrite** · **Synapse**

Opposite:
For the first two years of life, young humans are in the sensorimotor stage of development. During this time, a child learns about space, movement, balance, and the properties of things in its environment. Here, a young boy in the sensorimotor stage crawls to a door, focuses on the knob, and then stands up to touch and explore it.

is synthesized. All of this information is stored in memory. We now have learned the sound of the word *cat*, what it stands for, and what the word looks like. When someone says "cat" to us, asks us to read *cat*, or asks us to identify a cat, we can do it. We have learned the word *cat* and its meaning.

This explanation is a description of how one learns to read. Every kind of learning takes place in just that way. Information is constantly stored in the brain as memory until it is needed.

It takes the brain about 25 milliseconds (one millisecond is one thousandth of a second) to process a bit of information coming in from one of the senses. But for the learning-disabled, the processing time is much slower—about 300 milliseconds. This slow processing time can cause a variety of problems. One person might not be able to process certain sounds, might miss some sounds altogether, or might get them reversed. Another person might have a problem with the way letters look or are sounded. Information about shape and space might be poorly processed by the brain. The poorly processed information is stored in memory, and the learning-disabled person then has gaps in learning.

The Stages of Learning
Learning begins in a tiny baby as he or she learns to use his or her body. With motor control as the foundation, learning proceeds step by step with the next three skills—perception and memory, language, and thinking. If the individual misses one of these steps, a learning

disability is the result. These four steps—or stages—are
referred to as the sensorimotor stage, the preoperational
stage, the concrete operations stage, and the formal
operations stage.

The sensorimotor stage takes place during the first two years of a child's life. This is the time of discovering his or her world. The child touches, tastes, feels, hits, and pushes everything he or she can reach. The child is learning through his or her senses. The child hears the sounds and noises of the world and begins to use the throat and mouth to imitate those sounds. By his or her interaction with objects, the child learns about space— the position of objects in relation to his or her body. A child learns that an object can be in front of, behind, below, or above. As the child reaches out, he or she learns the qualities of color, hardness, and size.

The preoperational stage occurs from age two to seven. It is the time of acquiring language, of learning the symbols for the world that the child has discovered in the first stage. Perceptions—the signals about his or her world carried from the sense organs to the brain— become very important. Once the brain has processed a perception, the child finds the symbol for it. "Hot," says the child pointing to the stove. "I'm bigger than you," says the six-year-old to a classmate.

The concrete-operations stage covers ages 7 to 11. In this stage, an individual has the important tools for thinking—knowledge of objects in the world, perceptions, and language. He or she can organize perceptions and information stored in the brain and come to logical conclusions about objects. For example, if the red box is bigger than the blue box and the blue box is bigger than the yellow box, then the person can reason that the red box is bigger than the yellow box.

The formal-operations stage begins at about age 11. Adult powers of reasoning, or thinking, are developed during this time. Instead of a person's mental activity focusing on what is observed, thoughts originate in the brain and are tested by observations. For example, a child has already noticed that birds use wings to fly. What he or she now starts to explore is how birds use wings to fly. By using observations of a bird, the person may form a theory, or an idea, of how wings help a bird fly. A child will then progress to abstract thinking, considering such questions as: What is air? What is movement? How are people like birds? Soon the individual is ready to deal with such questions as: Why do things fall down instead of up? What makes the weather? Why is grass green? Using logic, the person begins to make good decisions about his or her actions, where at an earlier age an action was performed without a

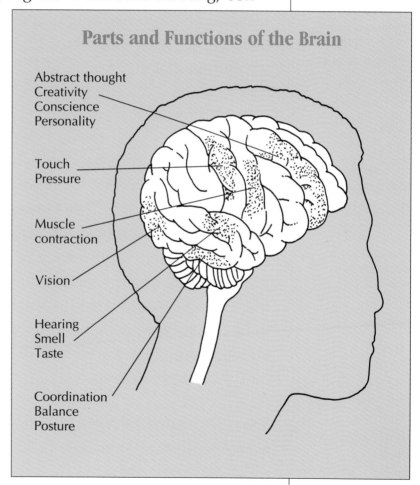

Parts and Functions of the Brain

Abstract thought
Creativity
Conscience
Personality

Touch
Pressure

Muscle
contraction

Vision

Hearing
Smell
Taste

Coordination
Balance
Posture

thought of the results. At age 3, a child would run into the street without thinking, but an 11-year-old looks before crossing.

Identifying Learning Problems

Scientists have determined many of the things that place someone at risk for learning disabilities. While not all the risk factors are known, the following have been identified: premature birth, poor nutrition of a pregnant mother and of the baby after birth, an illness or infection of a pregnant mother, smoking and drug use by a pregnant mother, and various possible hereditary factors. No one knows exactly how all of these factors affect the brain. There are, however, effective ways to help people with learning problems.

The first step in helping the learning-disabled is to diagnose them, to find the specific problems that are causing their disability. Doctors and teachers examine a child for four basic skills—motor control, perception of sensory information and memory, language (reading, writing, listening, and speaking), and thinking. Once the problem skill area has been found, the student can be helped to master that skill. Doctors and teachers prefer to begin working with a young child because the longer children struggle with their learning processes, the harder they are to help.

Development of Motor Skills

Many doctors and teachers believe that learning to move the body is the best way to help an individual

Sports and other physical activities are valuable ways for people to develop good motor skills. By concentrating and competing, participants also gain a valuable sense of self-confidence that is very important for learning.

sharpen those perceptions needed for other kinds of learning. But what is the link—exactly how does seeing the floor or sensing the space around the body help one learn to read? That question is still open to debate. One teacher has designed a physical-education program intended to help students learn to read. Games require that the students run or walk over large letters. The program also includes games in which the students must focus their attention. It is hoped that learning to focus attention during a game can be transferred to focusing attention on reading. This teacher, as well as others, believe that learning to use the body well—in order to ride a bicycle, to participate in sports, to play games— makes people feel better about themselves. When a person feels self-confident, it can carry over into his or her efforts to learn such subjects as reading and math.

There are children who have problems performing basic motor functions. In such cases, teachers design special programs to help them overcome their disabilities. Sets of motor-improving activities focus on three basic goals: learning to use the entire body; learning the body parts; and learning to move the hands, fingers, and eyes efficiently. Understanding the skills that need building in learning-disabled people helps one to better understand how these disabilities affect people in their daily lives.

Gross-motor activities involve all the body's muscles. Teachers work at helping learning-disabled students to learn to move all parts of the body in relation to each other, to gravity, and to the environment. Movements become smooth, and the child learns how his or her body fits into the space surrounding him or her. Children with gross-motor problems have trouble with such things as:

• walking straight and curved paths and walking backward and sideways.

• imitating animal movements, jumping, galloping and skipping.

• walking between the rungs of a ladder placed flat on the floor.

• crawling through an obstacle course containing boxes, chairs, and tables.

• lying on the floor and moving their arms and legs separately and together.

• walking forward and backward on a narrow board, in addition to walking on the board and pausing to pick up objects or drop objects into containers.

• doing jumping jacks—jumping and putting feet wide apart while clapping the hands over the head.

Body-image activities can help people with gross-motor problems by helping them to better sense the location of body parts. Body-image building activities often include:

• pointing to body parts while the eyes are closed.

• imitating the activities of a certain occupation, such as driving a bus.

• copying the movements of an instructor.

• following an instructor's verbal directions—"Put your left hand on your right knee."

Fine-motor activities help people control and use the small muscles of the hands, fingers, and eyes. In this way, individuals learn to coordinate what they see with what they do. This is called eye-hand coordination. Activities that build fine-motor skills include:

• throwing and catching balloons, sponges, bean-bags; rolling balls, bouncing balls, and throwing them against walls; playing video games and playing jacks.

• copying designs onto paper, folding paper into shapes, and lacing yarn through holes in cardboard.

• connecting dots to make pictures; drawing shapes with both hands; writing letters and numbers.

• following the movement of a pencil or the light of a flashlight with the eyes, and quickly shifting the gaze from one target to another and then back again.

Children who have memory and perception problems have trouble correctly processing and registering the sounds they hear and the things they see.

Problems with Perception and Memory

Tony was a forgetful seven-year-old who often set out to do one thing and ended up doing another. If his mother asked him to go upstairs, change into his play clothes, and bring her a sweater, Tony would go upstairs and appear an hour later in the same clothes and without the sweater. Tony wasn't being disobedient. He had trouble sorting out his mother's words from other sounds, and he couldn't remember most of what he heard. And so, when Tony got upstairs, he played with his toy tank for a while, watched the dog next door from his window, and then went back downstairs. Only after a lot of scolding and reminding did Tony finally get his clothes changed. It was a big job for him. There was so much for him to remember—tying and untying, buttoning, deciding which was the front of his shirt and pants. And he had to ignore the toy tank and the dog next door.

Tony's memory was so bad, he didn't know the days of the week in order or the alphabet. Tony also had trouble understanding what he heard. When he heard a car horn, he thought he was hearing a firecracker.

Tony is learning-disabled. His memory is poor, and although his hearing is normal, he can't hear sounds properly. Hearing, like vision, touch, smell, and taste, is one of the senses that provides us with information about the world around us. Perception and memory work hand in hand to help us learn. Perceptions traveling to different parts of the brain are stored as memory. A sound—for example, the bark of a dog—stimulates nerves of the ear. Neurons carry impulses to the brain, and the sound of the dog bark is heard or perceived by the person. Recognizing new perceptions depends on memory. Once we have heard the bark of a dog, it is stored as memory. The next time we hear that sound, our brain calls on its memory of sounds. The sound is matched to that of a dog bark, and we recognize the sound. It works the same for the other senses. We perceive the sight of a dog, the smell of roses, the taste of pizza, and the feel of hot and cold in the same way. We rely on our memory for these perceptions.

Perception

Perceptions are received through our sense organs. Each kind of perception is called a modality. Visual modality, auditory modality, tactile modality, and kinesthetic modality (muscle feeling) are the modalities involved in learning. Most of us find that one modality

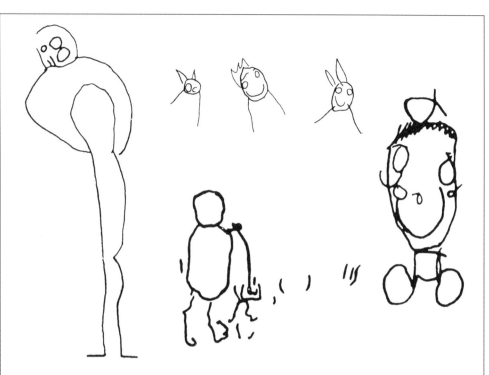

Visual-perception problems often cause difficulties with motor functions as well. These drawings of people, done by children with visual-perception problems, show a lack of control during the drawing process.

serves us better than our other ones. For example, some people may learn best by listening, but others may learn best by reading. This situation is exaggerated for the learning-disabled. They may find that none of their modalities are strong enough to make up for the one that is especially poor. For example, some people remember words by picturing them in their minds. They can match shapes and written words, but they cannot learn words to songs that they hear. Their visual modality works well, but their auditory modality does not. It is just the opposite for people who can remember verbal messages but cannot remember shapes that they see.

Visual perception   Good visual perception is important for the person who is learning to read or develop other skills. Some learning-disabled people cannot see words as separate items. Others cannot tell one letter

from another. They may recognize, for example, that the letters *b*, *d*, and *p* are all made up of lines and circles, but they cannot see that there are variations among these letters. Still others may not be able to recognize the different shapes, patterns, or objects.

Visual perception can be improved by exercises that help children focus on the differences between objects and symbols. Some common visual-skill-building exercises include:

• copying patterns or designs, using colored blocks or beads on a string.

• assembling jigsaw puzzles.

• matching drawings of certain shapes and objects and then doing the same exercise with letters and words.

• playing letter bingo, covering each letter on a card when it is called.

Auditory perception Good auditory perception is necessary to distinguish differences in sounds and words. Learning-disabled children may have trouble putting sounds together to form words, a skill important in learning to read. Poor auditory perception can interfere with the ability to remember what is heard.

To strengthen auditory perception, teachers will often ask students to:

• close their eyes and identify sounds. Sounds can be recorded, or they can be sounds such as using a stapler, closing a book, opening a window, eating an apple, or shaking something, such as sand in a jar.

• close their eyes and count repetitive sounds, such as the bouncing of a ball or tapping of a pencil.

• close their eyes and point to the source of a sound.

• search for a hidden object that makes a sound, such as a ticking clock.

• select from a group of spoken words the one that begins with the same letter as another word. Example: Select from the words *work, dance,* and *lake* the one that begins with the same letter as the word *dog.*

• select words that rhyme.

Tactile perception The learning-disabled may have problems with touch and kinesthetic (muscle feeling) perceptions. Knowing the feel and touch of objects is another way we learn about our world.

In order to help learning-disabled children to strengthen their tactile skills, teachers will ask them to do various touch and feel exercises. The children may be asked to:

Tactile perception means being able to recognize the feel and touch of objects.

- feel a variety of surfaces, wet objects, and foods.
- feel different shapes, objects that have different temperatures and different weights.
- close their eyes and identify a shape or figure that another person traces on the palm of their hand.
- identify objects in a bag by their feel.

Transferring information Some learning-disabled people may use all the modalities well but have trouble transferring information from one modality to another. For example, a person may know what a word looks like but cannot put the sight and the sound of the word together. He or she may be able to read the word *book* but may be unable to say it or write it.

Overloading the senses Other learning-disabled individuals suffer an overload of modalities. These people cannot deal with information coming into all modalities at once. A typical reading lesson will bombard all modalities with different aspects of a word. A student will see the word, see a picture of what the word means, hear the word, and must then spell and write the word. This approach is confusing to the learning-disabled whose modalities are overloaded or unable to process so much varying information at once.

Seeing the whole and the parts   There are certain people who cannot perceive both the whole and the parts of an object at the same time. They will therefore have a lot of trouble reading, since they will be unable to switch from seeing each letter in a word to seeing the word as a whole. Reading means seeing whole words as well as detecting small differences in words such as *dish* and *disk*.

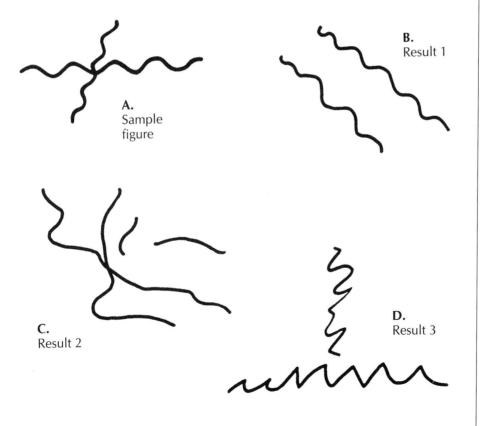

A.
Sample
figure

B.
Result 1

C.
Result 2

D.
Result 3

Many learning-disabled people have difficulty perceiving the parts of an object and then the whole object itself. This problem, called dissociation, can be seen in the drawings of three children who were asked to copy the lines they saw in figure A. The children saw the lines but could not properly see how the lines related to each other.

Memory

There are three stages in the memory process. First the information must be received and *registered* properly. The proper reception of information depends on the correct operation of the nerve impulses traveling from the sense organs to the brain. Then the information must be *stored*. Last of all, it must be *retrieved*, or re-called. Learning-disabled children may have problems with one or all of these stages because they lack the memory for certain things. Obviously they do remember many things, or they would not be able to function at all.

Registration is the first stage of memory. It involves receiving bits of information that are stored in short-term memory. The short-term-memory system is limited to a small amount of information. If the contents are not renewed through frequent repetition, they will quickly be lost. For example, if a student memorizes a bunch of facts just for a test, the information will fade from short-term memory soon after the test is over.

Storage of information in long-term memory occurs when people have understood and learned information over an extended time period. For example, students in a social studies class doing a unit on Africa may quickly forget incidental details, such as the names of Africa's capital cities, but those aspects of Africa that are dis-cussed throughout the unit—the people, the climate, the economy—will be retained in long-term memory. Information in long-term memory usually remains there for a lifetime.

The Stages of Memory

Stage 1: Registration
In the first stage, known as registration, information is perceived and understood. It is then retained in a short-term memory system that seems to be very limited in the amount of material it can store at one time. Unless refreshed by constant repetition, the contents of short-term memory are lost within minutes, to be replaced by other material.

Stage 2: Storage
If information is important enough, it may be transferred into the long-term memory, where the process of storage involves associations with words or meanings, with the visual imagery evoked by it, or with other experiences, such as smell or sound.

Stage 3: Retrieval
The final stage is retrieval, or recall, in which information stored at an unconscious level is brought, at will, into the conscious mind. The reliability of recall depends on how well the material was coded at Stage 2.

Retrieval, or recall, is the last stage of memory. At this stage, information that has been stored is brought into the conscious mind as it is needed. For example, you are calling on your memory of words when you read this sentence.

There is no way to improve memory. However, there are exercises that will make memory more efficient at storing and retrieving information. Exercises that strengthen storage and retrieval can include:

• giving verbal assignments, such as "Draw a blue square. Draw a red line under it. Draw a black line from the right hand end of the line to the upper left hand corner of the square."

• reading sentences aloud and asking students to repeat them.

• reading a story and having students retell it.

• asking students to look out of the window and describe the objects they see.

• placing different shapes, such as triangles, circles, and squares, in a particular order; covering them; and asking students to place a second set of objects in the same order.

Problems
with Perception
and Memory

27

Language disorders are the most common kind of learning disability. Often, these problems require the strengthening of auditory and motor capabilities. Here, a boy listens to and then follows auditory commands given through headphones.

Language Disorders

The following people exhibit their language disorders in different ways:

- Four-year-old Tina has not talked yet.
- Todd is nine years old and cannot read or write.
- Three-year-old Cindy cannot understand simple requests, such as "Sit down and drink your milk."
- Although he is in first grade, Randy still uses baby talk. He says such things as, "Me want the ball" and "Randy dog name Rex."
- Kim, five years old, cannot think of the words she wants to use. She uses *thing* for many words and sometimes gets her words wrong. She says "big" when she means "little," and "early" when she means "late."

Each of these people has a different kind of language disorder, the most common type of learning disability.

Language-disabled people have serious problems with speaking, listening, reading, writing, and spelling. Some of these problems may be related to motor disabilities or may be the result of difficulties with perception and memory.

What Is Language?

Language is human speech, either spoken or written. It involves mastering the use of words as symbols for things, actions, ideas, and events. In this way, people learn about each another and the world in which they live. Communication plays a key role in learning, thinking, and controlling one's environment. Imagine what it would be like if you couldn't ask for food, recognize a cry for help, perceive what an object is, or understand why something is happening. You would be cut off from the world around you.

Language has a set of systems or parts. These are the word sounds (phonics), the meaning of parts of words (morphology), the word order within sentences (syntax), the meaning of language (semantics), and the meaning of the sound patterns of words (intonation). People with language disorders have problems with one or more of these systems.

Phonics: Some language-disabled people cannot put certain sounds together in order to form a word. They hear the sounds, but their brain is unable to process them properly. For example, they cannot combine the sounds of the letters *d, o, g,* to produce the sound of the word *dog.*

Spoken language is one of our most basic means of communication and a major part of the way we interact with the world around us.

Morphology: The language-disabled may not be able to understand plurals. For example, they may not understand that the word *cat* means just one cat, while the addition of an *s* to the word means more than one cat. These people may not understand how to use the past tense of a verb or the exceptions to the rules of grammar.

Syntax: The language-disabled have trouble forming sentences. For example, they may not understand that the sentences "Dad is home" and "Is Dad home?" have different meanings. To these people, the sentences "The truck is followed by the car" and "The truck follows the car," are understood to mean the same thing.

Semantics: The language-disabled may have difficulties with the meaning of words. People with such problems do not share the same understanding of words as most others and, therefore, do not understand much of what they read and hear.

Intonation: A language-disabled child may not understand that emphasizing sounds or words adds a certain meaning. For example, if someone says "Come here" angrily, it means one thing. Saying "Come here" gently means another thing. The language-disabled who do not understand the rules of intonation may speak in a singsong way, putting no emphasis on any word.

How Language Is Learned

Scientists do not really understand how we acquire language. It is believed that we are born with the ability to learn the language we hear spoken around us when we are very young. Both the words we hear and the experiences we have help us understand and use words and sentences. Children who hear English as infants will learn English when they speak. Those who grow up hearing Spanish or Chinese will learn those languages.

The importance of learning language at an early age can be found in the case of Victor. At 12 years old, he was found living alone in the woods of southern France in 1800. Victor was a wild boy who had little contact with humans. He neither spoke nor understood speech and was never able to learn after he was found. His lack of experience with language as a child prevented him from ever learning it later in life.

We develop language in steps. As babies we listen; then we begin to speak. Next come reading and writing. Listening and reading involve drawing information into the brain. Speaking and writing are output skills, which involve producing information in the brain and sending it out. There are two basic kinds of language— oral and written.

Oral Language

Oral language involves listening and speaking, the first two skills we learn before receiving any formal language training in school.

Listening is not the same as hearing. Hearing involves detecting sounds. Listening, on the other hand, means using the brain to organize and make some sense of those sounds. Since listening is the way we begin to learn language, it is the very foundation of language.

Training and practice can improve various listening skills. Teachers use a number of exercises to help the language-disabled improve their ability to use language effectively. Some of these exercises were discussed in the previous chapter. Other listening exercises include:

- learning the sounds of letters by comparing the sounds of words.
- learning the meanings of words by comparing spoken words with pictures, actions, and gestures.
- learning words in certain classifications, such as foods, toys, and animals.
- learning to understand sentences by filling in missing words and by following simple directions.
- learning location words, such as *inside, over,* and *behind*, by placing objects inside, over, or behind other objects.
- learning to listen for details by retelling a set of directions.
- listening to a story and then giving it a title that tells what the story is about.
- listening to the beginning of an exciting story and then making up an ending.

Speaking begins with the first cry of the newborn baby. For about 9 months, the baby babbles, gurgles, and coos. Then the baby starts to experiment with the sounds of letters and intonations. Sometime between 12 and 18 months of age, the child says his or her first word. The child is copying sounds and words that he or she hears. From that point, the child starts using short sentences. By the time the child is six years old, he or she has mastered the speaking of language and can say and understand about 24,000 words.

People with a language disorder do not progress in these stages. They may have problems with one or more of the five language systems that provide the meanings of sounds and words. The speaking-disabled need training in developing a listening vocabulary (knowing the meaning of words they hear), producing sounds, learning the morphology of language (meanings of the sounds and word parts), and forming sentences. To strengthen speaking skills, teachers will ask their students to:

• name objects in the classroom or outside the window. Learn other words from pictures. Play games such

A baby's first wails are also its first expression of spoken language. As a child develops, it is able to master the different forms of language on increasingly complex levels.

as department store, restaurant, or hardware store. A student pretends to be a customer and orders certain items. A student pretending to be a clerk finds pictures of these items and names them as he or she gives them to the customer.

- match words such as *bread* and *butter* and *bee* and *flower*.
- exercise the speech muscles by smiling, chewing, swallowing, whistling, and laughing.
- say words as the teacher says them, copying the mouth movements and the use of the tongue.
- practice using singular and plural nouns with the proper form of the verb. For example, "The boy is running" and "The boys are running."
- make a variety of sentences from one sentence. For example, from the sentence "I can't find the book," make a question—"Did you find the book?"
- play a detective game in which questions are asked about a hidden object until it is found.
- practice speaking skills by pretending to speak on the phone, telling a story, pretending to be a television reporter, describing an activity such as getting dressed for school, and answering questions.

Written Language
Written language involves reading the printed word, learning to put down on paper written symbols (the alphabet), and using those symbols in words, sentences, and paragraphs in accordance with the rules of spelling and grammar.

Reading is the basic tool of learning. Failure in school quite often results from the inability to read. Students who have trouble learning to read may have a disorder called dyslexia. Dyslexic children also have difficulty writing and spelling.

Learning to read proceeds in stages. The first stage is reading readiness, which begins when a baby is born. Listening, babbling, learning to use his or her body, learning to speak, and interacting with the world, the child is developing a concept of sounds and words. In the second stage, the child begins to match the sounds of spoken words with written words. On that trium-phant day when the child reads his or her first word, he or she discovers that written words are the code for parts

Understanding written language is essential to learning. Reading and understanding what is read involves the use of visual skills as well as perception and memory.

Language Disorders

A learning-disabled boy works with letter tiles to strengthen reading skills. By putting words together letter by letter, a student can better understand the construction and meaning of written language.

of the world. Words, the child soon discovers, are talk written down.

The third stage involves developing a vocabulary of words that are recognized on sight. A student learns how to read unfamiliar words by sounding out parts of the word. By stage four, a student has often become so good at reading that he or she reads for pleasure. In the library, the student will pick out books about children, animals, or other favorite subjects and enjoy reading them. In the fifth stage, a student learns to read in order to gain knowledge. This involves reading, while at the same time understanding what is read. In addition, the student learns how to read a wide variety of materials from science to history to English.

As a first step in helping the reading-disabled, the teacher examines the student's progress through the stages of reading and determines his or her skills. For example, can the student analyze words by recognizing letter sounds, and can that student then blend those sounds and syllables to form words? Does the student have perceptual or memory problems? Once the student's problems are determined, then he or she can be put into a reading program that works to use the individual's strengths and helps build up weak skills.

If, for example, the student has good auditory perception, he or she is put into a reading program that emphasizes matching the sound with the written form of letters. Such a program strengthens not only reading but also speaking and writing. The student tells stories to the teacher, who writes them down. Then the student and the teacher read the story together. The student learns that the spoken word can be written and then read. Another reading program for students with good auditory perception involves the student reading along with the teacher. Here, the interactions among hearing, speaking, and reading are stressed.

The individual who begins to use all senses well may be put into a program in which he or she uses all the senses to learn words. The student says the word, traces it with a finger, sees the word, and hears the teacher say it.

Writing is the last language skill learned. It is the most complicated and is based on skills that have already been mastered—listening, speaking, and reading. Writing requires putting an idea into words, forming the letters, and spelling the words.

Developing handwriting is the way acquiring written language begins. It requires coordinated effort from the muscles that move the eyes, arm, hand, and fingers. The shapes of letters and words must be clearly perceived, and that information must be sent to the muscles used for writing. Writing-disabled children have trouble with one or more of the three skills that are involved in writing—muscular coordination, perception of letters and words, and transfer of information from the visual mode to the muscles.

A number of exercises can help the writing-disabled improve their skills. Some of these include:

• practicing drawing shapes, lines, letters, and numbers on a chalkboard; finger-painting; and using the finger or a pointed stick to make shapes in a flat pan of sand or cornmeal.

• learning to hold a pencil between the thumb and middle finger, with the index finger guiding.

• tracing shapes, lines, letters, and numbers on transparent paper placed on top of a guide.

• learning to write letters and understanding how they are constructed. Spacing and slant of the letters is also practiced.

Spelling requires that the individual be able to read words, analyze the parts of the words, understand the sounds in the words, see the word in his or her mind, and write the word. The student who has trouble spelling must be tested to determine if he or she can spell words out loud, pronounce words properly, sound out the letters, spell syllables, write letters properly, and distinguish different sounds (auditory perception) and sights (visual perception).

If auditory and visual perception are found to be poor, the student will most likely be asked to do some of the perception and memory exercises described in the previous chapter. This will help the student to decode and remember letter sounds as well as to perceive and remember what the word looks like.

A typical spelling program uses the senses of vision, hearing, and touch to teach the student to spell. To help the learning-disabled strengthen their skills, teachers will ask them to do exercises that combine various senses at once. Some of these exercises include:

- look at a word, say it, and use it in a sentence.
- say a word, then the syllables, spell it, trace the letters with a finger.
- close your eyes, and picture a word in your mind. Then spell the word out loud. Open your eyes to see if the word was spelled correctly. If not, try again.
- write a word from memory, and check to see if it is right. If correct, write it two more times.

Once the skills of handwriting and spelling are mastered, a student, faced with a writing task, needs something to write about—an idea. Ideas come from experience—field trips, stories, conversations. The teacher begins by asking the students to tell about an experience. The teacher writes it down as the students tell it. As the teacher writes, students learn about rules of capitalization, spelling, and punctuation. Students copy what the teacher has written and then, with the teacher's help, practice rewriting the story on their own.

Children with writing or spelling problems often have trouble with visual skills, as well as problems with motor functions, perception, and memory.

Difficulties with thinking
and reasoning affect a
person's ability to learn
new concepts and to
solve problems like
putting together a
jigsaw puzzle.

Thinking Problems

The following young people exhibit thinking problems in various ways:

- Fifteen-month-old Brenda sits quietly in a chair for more than an hour. She doesn't move and pays no attention to the doll her mother has given her. When the doll falls on the floor, Brenda does not notice.

- Michael, who is five years old, cannot button his jacket, or tie his shoelaces. His new tricycle sits in the garage because he can't learn to pedal it. Michael can't jump or hop on one foot. He speaks well and can copy a circle and a square, but he can't color inside the lines.

- In science class, 13-year-old Josh watches an experiment. The teacher has two glasses of water. The glasses are the same size, and the water comes to the same level in each glass. The teacher pours all the water from one glass into another glass that is taller and narrower. Now there are two different-sized glasses of water. "Which one has the most water?" asks the teacher. Josh answers, "The tall one." He does not understand that the amount of water that was once in a glass of one size and now is in another size glass is still the same amount.

Brenda, Michael, and Josh are behind in the kind of thinking skills they should have for their ages. At 15 months, Brenda should be on the go, investigating all that is around her. Michael should be able to understand his relationship to the world around him and be able to use his body better. Josh, at 13, should be able to understand the relationship of size to volume.

What Is Thinking?

Thinking means using knowledge to develop ideas and do new things—to produce something new, such as a new machine or a poem. You are thinking when you decide there is a problem and find a way to solve that problem. Here are some examples:

• A mother hears her child fall down the steps. She discovers that his arm is twisted strangely. That is the problem. Her solution is to put him in the car and take him to the hospital.

• You are getting dressed for school. It is cold outside. That is the problem. Your solution is to wear warm clothes.

• Your big sister is vacuuming the rug, when the vacuum cleaner suddenly begins to make a loud, clunking noise. That is the problem. Your sister takes the bottom of the vacuum cleaner nozzle apart and removes a large paper clip that was tangled and trapped inside the rollers. That is the solution.

What are the specific problems of learning-disabled individuals who have difficulty thinking? Usually, these people haven't progressed through the four stages of learning discussed in Chapter 1 (sensorimotor, preoperational, concrete-operations, and formal-operations stages). This is because they lack certain skills: receiving information correctly from the world by way of the sense organs; organizing, categorizing, and storing information in memory; communicating information through language or action; and determining the effect of behavior on others and the surroundings. These skills work together, so if individuals have a problem with one such skill, they can't use the others properly either.

Concept Formation

The difficulties that some learning-disabled people have with thinking can be traced to their inability to form concepts. Concepts are general ideas about things. For example, roundness is a concept about such objects as balls, plates, and pencils. A kind of object—a chair, for example—is also a concept. A lounge chair, a kitchen chair, or a stuffed chair are all chairs. A group of objects, like furniture, is another concept, of which a chair, as well as a table and bed are a part. Other concepts, unlike chair and furniture, can't be seen or touched. Love, fairness, and bravery are examples of this kind of concept. Understanding concepts does not simply mean knowing the meanings of individual words. It also enables a person to form ideas about observations— "That was a brave act." "That has four legs, a seat, and a back. It is a chair."

Teachers help learning-disabled students develop concepts by taking them on field trips and providing them with pictures, books, and other information about many kinds of things. Then the students are taught how to evaluate, classify, and summarize the things they learn about. For example, on a trip to the zoo, they learn to classify all animals that have feathers and wings as birds. In a book about a police officer or a firefighter, they learn about bravery.

Thinking Skills

There are two kinds of thinking skills, verbal and nonverbal. Verbal skills have to do with language— listening, reading, speaking, and writing. We use language to think—it helps us to organize information, and it is used to develop ideas and actions. It also works the other way—as thinking improves, language improves, too. Nonverbal skills are understanding facial expressions and gestures, assembling puzzles, remembering shapes, understanding how shapes fit together, and thinking in numbers.

Arithmetic is an example of a nonverbal skill. Many of the skills that learning-disabled students lack go back to the basics of learning about space, shape, time, distance, and quantity. Once these students have been put through the exercises described in the previous chapters,

and Emily sold 25. What
the total number of tickets that th
two girls sold?

2) There are 14 girls and 12 boys i
Bill's math class. How many students
there altogether?

125
+26

they can be taken step-by-step through the solving of a problem. Another way that students learn to problem-solve is to encourage them to ask questions about the problem before guiding them to the answers. This way, students learn that thinking is often just that—asking questions and answering them.

Reading comprehension, or understanding what is read, is an example of a verbal thinking skill. As readers decode symbols into words, they must understand not only the words in the sentences but also the ideas that those sentences represent. Readers must evaluate the

Math skills are nonverbal skills that involve problem solving with numbers and symbols instead of letters and words.

Reading and understanding what we read are essential parts of functioning in the world. The written word is used for countless things in our everyday surroundings so that people can communicate most effectively with one another.

ideas as they go along and find meanings and ideas that the writer has hinted at. This is sometimes called "reading between the lines." For example, the following sentence about a boy who has just been scolded—"The boy looked at the floor"—tells readers indirectly that the boy was ashamed or timid without writing those exact words.

Readers must also develop an idea of the overall theme of a story in order to understand meaning. For example, in a story a man keeps trying and failing, then one day succeeds. The theme is "Never give up." And finally, readers should get new ideas and understandings from what they read. In one story, a girl earns a trip to camp by selling the most cookies. This might spark an idea for the reader to pursue something that is similar: "Maybe I could earn money by selling those yarn rabbits that I learned to make."

Reading comprehension can be strengthened in a number of ways, including:

• making up a title for a story or a group of paragraphs that have just been read.

• putting certain events from a story in the order in which they occurred.

• asking what new things were learned from a story.

• comparing and analyzing newspaper stories on the same subject, looking for logic and fairness; or reading advertisements to determine if claims and promises make sense.

• asking questions such as, "What do I think about what I've just read? Why do I think that? Can I prove it?"

Learning disabilities can cause great emotional pain and anxiety in those affected. Often, these feelings cause students to lose interest in learning, to feel inferior, and to give up on their hopes of learning or understanding.

Behavioral Problems

Mr. Rivera's class was hard at work on an arithmetic assignment when eight-year-old Jamie stood up and called out, "How do you like my new shirt? I got it for my birthday." Then Jamie left his seat and ran to watch the fish in their tank. Mr. Rivera ordered Jamie back to his seat. A minute later, Jamie was out of his seat again, asking Jessica for her eraser. Back in his seat again, Jamie wriggled about and dropped his pencil. While bending over to pick it up, he fell. When the class ended, Jamie turned in a sloppy arithmetic paper on which he had done only one of the problems. At recess no one would play with Jamie because he refused to follow game rules and would stomp and scream if he couldn't have his way.

Shortly after returning home, Jamie would do such things as knock over a lamp, spill milk, step on the cat's tail, and start a fight with his little brother.

Jamie realized the effect his actions had on others, but he just couldn't help himself. He couldn't stay still, and he couldn't pay attention to anything for more than a few seconds. Jamie felt very sad. It hurt him that other children wouldn't play with him and that he couldn't seem to do anything right. How he wished that the teacher or his dad would praise him. He felt worthless and sometimes struck out at those around him.

Jamie has attention deficit hyperactivity disorder (ADHD), a behavioral problem. He is also suffering from social problems because of his behavior, and this has produced additional behavioral problems.

Monica was doing well in her lessons at school, but because of her behavior she was a social failure. She laughed when others made mistakes in class. When the class read a sad story, Monica found it funny. A funny story made her sad. Monica also said what she thought, like "You're fat" and "Your mother is ugly."

Her classmates avoided Monica, and this hurt her feelings. In an attempt to get them to like her, Monica would sometimes hug and kiss other children for no reason. Other times she would get angry and start a fight with someone who had hurt her feelings by ignoring her. These actions just made her classmates dislike her even more.

Monica has trouble sensing the feelings of others. This problem is considered a learning disability. It stems from Monica's difficulty in learning how she fits into the world. When she was younger, she couldn't point to her feet, nose, arms, and other body parts. When looking at a family picture, she had no image of her body and didn't recognize herself. Even at nine, Monica was always losing her way in the school halls. She would often bump into things and didn't know right from left. Because she couldn't sense her own place in the space around her, she couldn't understand the place of others and their relationship to her.

Jamie and Monica both suffer from behavioral problems. Jamie's behavior prevents him from learning. Monica's behavior makes her seem strange and unkind

Students must have a proper sense of how they relate to others in order to function in society. Group projects and classroom assignments build and strengthen social skills that are much needed in the adult world.

to others. Because of their behavior, Jamie and Monica are social outcasts. They feel worthless and unloved, and they react with more objectionable behavior.

Attention Deficit Hyperactivity Disorder
The symptoms of attention deficit hyperactivity disorder (ADHD) are overactivity; the inability to pay attention, or concentrate; impulsiveness (acting without thinking); restlessness; sudden explosive behavior (rage); and irritability (being ill-tempered). In the past, ADHD was believed to be caused by minor brain damage. Then scientists developed the theory that particular foods, perhaps fluorescent lights, lead poisoning, or all three caused ADHD. Scientists now believe that ADHD is a collection of problems resulting from a number of different disorders. Included among these is a disease of a gland in the throat called the thyroid, sleep disorders, and several kinds of mental illnesses that affect a person's mood. The learning disabilities that were discussed in the previous chapters can also cause ADHD problems. People with ADHD problems may have one or more of these disorders.

Physicians can examine people to determine the cause of the ADHD problems. Thyroid disease, sleep disorders and mental illness can be treated with medicines and counseling. When learning disabilities are involved, however, the symptoms of ADHD interfere with overcoming the disability. In such cases, the basic problems—called distractibility, impulsivity, and hyperactivity—must be treated one by one.

Distractibility, or inattentiveness, refers to the inability to focus attention on important events or things. The minds of those who are easily distracted wander from one less important matter to another. To help such people focus their attention, a classroom or study area that is free of noise, other people, and other distractions must be provided. There, they must be given only one assignment at a time and must listen to instructions for an assignment through the earphones of a recorder. Background noise is gradually added to the directions. This helps the student learn to select important sounds from the many that they hear.

Impulsivity is characteristic of a person who takes sudden actions or says something without giving any prior thought or consideration to his or her words or deeds. For example, in the middle of a class, a student may blurt out some irrelevant idea, such as, "We're going to have pizza tonight for dinner." Teachers and parents can work with children to help them decrease their impulsivity. Doctors can also prescribe medicines to make these young people less impulsive.

Hyperactivity is a pattern of behavior among certain individuals who are constantly overactive. These people are full of energy and always on the go. Their overactive behavior is frequently worse when they are in a class-room or in some other kind of situation where there is much stimulation from the surrounding environment. Some hyperactive people can be taught to slow down and control their movements. Sometimes they can also be treated with medicines that have a calming effect.

Often, hyperactive individuals don't realize how disturbing and distracting their behavior can be to those around them. Once they are able to understand this, however, reminders by teachers and parents can help hyperactive people to control their constant actions.

Poor Social Perception

People with poor social perception can't perform tasks independently; can't judge the moods and attitudes of others; and can't judge the mood of a situation, such as the happy atmosphere of a party or the sadness of a funeral. They lack feeling for others and are continually saying the wrong things; seem to lack normal emotions; and have a lot of difficulty forming bonds with other people. The results are hurtful for such individuals, since others turn away from them, denying them the very thing that they need the most—understanding how to care about other people.

Some scientists believe that this disorder begins in the baby who is born with a tendency to avoid the new or unfamiliar. Such a baby is extremely shy, and any kind of exposure to something new can often be stressful. The baby doesn't explore his or her world, doesn't try out new toys, and as a result doesn't learn how to solve problems. This inability to solve problems extends to learning about other people.

Individuals with poor social perception usually need training in four different areas: body image, or perception of self; sensitivity to other people; understanding social situations; and social maturity.

Body image is something that children can be trained to understand by comparing the body parts on a doll with their own, by assembling puzzles, and by completing pictures of people. Children can learn how body parts interact with space by imitating the moves of pictures or videos of other people. With the assistance of a teacher or a parent, they can prepare a scrapbook, containing photos of themselves, their families, and their pets; a list of their favorite things; and stories describing their experiences. Doing this helps such children to get a concrete view of their image.

Sensitivity to others can be developed in young people if they are taught to understand the unspoken language of gestures (body language) and facial expressions. They can learn gestures by watching videos of people waving good-bye and motioning to other people. Crucial to learning gestures is gaining an inner understanding of what they mean. To do this, children need to imitate both the gesture and the expected response.

People with poor social perception feel left out and lonely. Often, low self-esteem and an inability to connect with others will make these problems even worse.

Behavioral Problems

Observing pictures of people with sad, happy, angry, pained, loving, surprised, and frightened looks on their faces helps individuals understand facial expressions. As with gestures, it is very important that young people develop an inner understanding of the meaning of facial expressions. To do this, Polaroid (instant) pictures are taken of these individuals when they are looking sad, for example. By looking at the photos, they will be able to see what their faces look like when they feel this emotion.

Once children have learned facial expressions, they can try out their knowledge in situations. For example, after examining a picture of a baby being given a toy, they can select from a set of pictures the expression the baby would have on his or her face. Pretending to do such things as mowing the lawn, setting the table, or combing one's hair helps children understand the body movements involved in various activities.

Social situations can be properly handled by young people if they are trained to evaluate pictures or videos of social situations. Students can discuss with a teacher the results of the actions they saw in the film, and they might try to answer such questions as: "How would a person feel if someone called him or her fat?" "How would a person feel if someone made an angry face when being introduced?"

Social maturity means being independent, reaching out, and understanding the results of actions. Young people can begin to gain independence by planning parties, trips, and meetings. They can also learn to prepare and read maps so they can feel comfortable about exploring. In addition, they can participate in plays and write stories about what would happen if there were no rules of conduct. From there they can go on to make judgments about right and wrong.

What Courage and Help Can Achieve

The learning-disabled often suffer emotional problems as a result of their failure to learn. These problems involve their sense of worth and pride. Those around them—parents, teachers, classmates—may also have poor opinions of them. No one may ever say, "Good job" or "I'm proud of you."

One of the best ways that parents and teachers can help children with these behavior problems is to give them a taste of success. If learning-disabled people work toward a goal that can reasonably be achieved and are given advice and assistance along the way—including high praise upon success—they will feel better about themselves. Support and encouragement from teachers, family, and friends has helped many learning-disabled people accomplish wonderful things. Several individuals who are famous for great feats actually overcame their learning disabilities in order to distinguish themselves in the fields of sports, science, and the arts.

A number of world-famous leaders, such as President Woodrow Wilson, English prime minister Winston Churchill, and New York governor Nelson Rockefeller, are all thought to have suffered from learning disabilities. The great inventor Thomas Edison and scientist Albert Einstein both had severe problems with writing,

Acknowledged by most of the world as a true scientific genius, Albert Einstein was also known to have struggled with learning disorders. Here, he takes his oath of U.S. citizenship in 1940.

spelling, and reading. Renaissance master Leonardo da Vinci and sculptor Auguste Rodin are also believed by researchers and scholars to have had learning difficulties. Authors Walt Whitman, William Butler Yeats, Hans Christian Andersen, and Agatha Christie are known to have struggled with reading and learning, and Bruce Jenner, famous Olympic decathlon gold medalist, reportedly has a reading disorder.

The achievements of these people—and many others—show clearly that learning disabilities can be overcome. Their accomplishments prove that, with the proper help and guidance, learning-disabled people can learn to live successful, happy, and very productive lives.

Glossary

abstract thinking Thinking in terms of ideas rather than concrete objects.

attention deficit hyperactivity disorder (ADHD) A collection of behavioral problems that are characterized by constant activity and the inability to pay attention.

auditory modality The sense of the ears, which provides the perception of hearing.

body image The sense a person has of his or her body and how it fits into the surrounding space.

concept A general idea about a thing or an event.

distractibility The inability to focus attention.

dyscalculia The inability to learn mathematics.

dysgraphia The inability to write.

dyslexia The inability to read.

eye-hand coordination Matching the movement of the eyes with the use of the hands.

hyperactivity Excessive activity.

impulsivity Acting without thinking.

intonation Giving certain meanings to words or sentences through pronunciation and emphasis.

kinesthetic modality Muscle feeling.

memory Information stored in the brain.

modality An avenue of sensation, such as vision.

morphology The system of word-forming elements and processes in a language.

motor activity The use of the muscles of the body.

neuron A nerve cell.

neurotransmitter A chemical that sends messages from one neuron to another.

nucleus The unit at the center of a body cell.

perception Information from the senses received by the brain about a person's environment.

phonics The sounds of letters and words.

semantics The meaning of language.

social perception The ability to sense the feelings of others.

syntax The order of words used in sentences.

tactile modality The sense of the skin, which provides the perception of touch.

visual modality The sense of the eyes, which provides the perception of vision.

Further Reading

Almonte, Paul and Desmond, Theresa. *Learning Disabilities*. New York: Crestwood House, 1992.

August, Paul. *Brain Function*. New York: Chelsea House, 1988.

Facklam, Margery and Facklam, Howard. *Brain: Magnificent Mind Machine*. San Diego: Harcourt Brace Jovanovich, 1982.

Gallant, Roy A. *Memory: How It Works and How to Improve It*. New York: Four Winds, 1984.

Ireland, Karen. *Albert Einstein*. Morristown, New Jersey: Silver Burdett, 1989.

Knox, Jean. *Learning Disabilities*. New York: Chelsea House, 1989.

Landau, Elaine. *Dyslexia*. New York: Franklin Watts, 1991.

Marshall, Norman F. and Ripamonti, Aldo. *Leonardo da Vinci*. Morristown, New Jersey: Silver Burdett, 1990.

Mathers, Douglas. *Brain*. Mahwah, New Jersey: Troll, 1992.

Parker Steve. *Brain and Nervous System*. New York: Franklin Watts, 1991.

Parker, Steve. *Learning a Lesson: How You See, Think, and Remember*. New York: Franklin Watts, 1991.

Rodgers, Judith. *Winston Churchill*. New York: Chelsea House, 1986.

Savage, John F. *Dyslexia: Understanding Reading Problems*. New York: Julian Messner, 1985.

Index

Photo Credits:
P. 4: ©Doug Plummer/Photo Researchers, Inc.; p. 11: ©Stuart Rabinowitz/Blackbirch Graphics, Inc.; p. 15: ©Stephanie FitzGerald/Blackbirch Graphics, Inc.; p. 18: ©Jeff Isaac Greenberg/Photo Researchers, Inc.; p. 22: ©Jim Davis/Photo Researchers, Inc.; p. 24: ©David M. Grossman/Photo Researchers, Inc.; p. 28: ©Hank Morgan/Photo Researchers, Inc.; p. 31: Blackbirch Graphics, Inc.; p. 35: ©David M. Grossman/ Photo Researchers, Inc.; p. 37: ©Gaillard/Jerrican/Photo Researchers, Inc.; p. 38: ©Siu/Photo Researchers, Inc.; p. 41: ©Will and Deni McIntyre/Photo Researchers, Inc.; p. 42: ©Alex Bartel/Science Photo Library/Photo Researchers, Inc.; p. 47: ©Richard Hutchings/Photo Researchers, Inc.; p. 48: ©Stuart Rabinowitz/Blackbirch Graphics, Inc.; p. 50: ©Spencer Grant/Photo Researchers, Inc.; p. 53: ©Richard Hutchings/Photo Researchers, Inc.; p. 57: ©Stuart Rabinowitz/Blackbirch Graphics, Inc.; p. 60: National Archives.

Technical illustrations: ©Blackbirch Graphics, Inc.